Telephoning

your questions and answers

Josy Roberts

TROTMAN

About the Author

Josy Roberts has worked in administrative, marketing and management roles over the last 15 years for a variety of organisations, including family-owned small businesses, charities and major corporations. As well as the scars of experience she holds an honours degree in Sociology, a marketing certificate and Diploma in Management.

She believes strongly that the success of organisations and individuals – whatever they do – is based on communications skills and a professional approach, and with that the working day can and should be enjoyable.

This first edition published in 1998 in Great Britain by Trotman and Company Limited, 12 Hill Rise, Richmond, Surrey TW10 6UA
© Trotman and Company Limited 1998

British Library Cataloguing in Publication Data
A catalogue record for this book is available from the British Library
ISBN 0 85660 325 2

Printed and bound in Great Britain by Redwood Books

1. Why use the telephone?

The telephone is probably the most important business communication tool. Every business – including one-man-bands like window cleaners, accountants and freelance illustrators – relies on the telephone to keep in touch with their clients. Do you know of any business without a telephone? Handling telephone contact well makes the difference between selling products and services or losing customers.

The telephone is used to give and receive information. It has several advantages over other communication channels like letters, email, faxes or face-to-face meetings.

❑ The equipment is easy to use and uncomplicated – a handset and number keypad, which most people master by the age of six (although developing mastery of telephone usage takes a bit longer, as this book explains).

❑ It's interactive and immediate – specific questions can be answered instantly.

❑ It's personal and personalised. A telephone call is between two people and it can convey exactly the information a contact needs, at a time that is convenient.

❑ It's cheap. Despite call charges it is much less expensive to make a telephone call compared to the time taken to prepare and post a letter or attend a meeting.

❑ Appearance doesn't matter. You don't have to be in a swish office or dressed in an expensive suit to make a good impression.

Most people discover that throughout their lives using the telephone saves them time, and gets things done. Having lots of phone calls makes you feel popular and active – it is easy to get in touch, to share ideas and news, to keep all kinds of relationships going and to solve problems. 'It's good to talk' may sound like just a clever marketing slogan, but there is truth in it for business as well as social reasons.

On the flip side, telephone calls can be demanding and interrupting. They frequently mean it's necessary to reorganise work, or address new problems.

Why do I need to know about telephone skills at work?

Telephones are so much part of everyday life, especially workplaces, that it is inevitable you will need to use them. You will have to do some of the following using the phone:

- ❏ Find out information for a report, letter or project
- ❏ Arrange meetings
- ❏ Interest someone in your company's products or services
- ❏ Apply for a job
- ❏ Place an order or buy something
- ❏ Ask for help
- ❏ Deal with a customer's query
- ❏ Take an order for a product
- ❏ Convey important news
- ❏ Deal with a customer's complaint
- ❏ Solve a problem quickly.

Whatever type of work you do, it is likely you will need to use the phone to communicate with people outside your workplace. So it is important that you learn how to work on the telephone well – to do your own job, and to help in the success of your organisation.

What can go wrong on the telephone?

Telephone contact is so vital to business, and the phone itself is a simple and familiar object. So why do things go wrong and why are some people so scared of it?

Misunderstandings

Conversations that leave the caller and the receiver with different ideas – which causes confusion, and someone not getting what they expected.

Bad impressions

The caller or customer thinks less of the organisation or person after the phone call, and decides to contact somebody else to do business with.

Anger and upset

The conversation leaves someone with negative emotions – which cause stress.

Embarrassment

You end up feeling guilty, silly or inadequate because the conversation hasn't resulted in a successful outcome.

No wonder many people are afraid of using the phone. You don't know what will happen each time you pick up the receiver. It could be a delightful adventure or a hideous experience.

The uncertainty is compounded by the 'blindness' of telephones. You can't see the other person to pick up visual signals about their reaction. You can't see facial expressions or body language – to tell if they are bored, frustrated, interested, angry or amused.

You can't make eye contact to keep them concentrating on what you are saying. You can't lip read to make sure you get all the words they are saying.

However, picking up the receiver needn't be like jumping into a black hole. If you can learn basic skills for controlling telephone conversations they will work in your favour, helping you to do your job more efficiently and enjoyably.

2. What are the basics for using the telephone?

1. Be prepared. The Boy Scout motto is both succinct and apt. Be ready for a conversation when you answer the telephone or make a call – *before* you touch the handset.

2. Speak clearly. All the other person has to analyse is the sound of your voice. If you make it difficult or unpleasant they will soon get frustrated, which will immediately become a negative opinion.

3. Stick to the subject. Don't ramble or provide unnecessary detail. 'Of course Mr Plankton, I'll send you the information on our biological products straight away. It's a lovely brochure actually, all green and misty, with cute little pictures. My friend Flora has cut one up and made a super collage. Now I'm not sure what envelope is best…' Mr Plankton is likely to think you are close to a single cell amoebae in the evolutionary chain.

4. Develop your listening skills and write things down, and make sure you get the details right. 'Mrs Shatobryand, could you spell your surname for me please?'

5. Understand the different types of question and use questions to move the conversation forward.

6. Know how to use the equipment. Saying 'sorry, I can't transfer you, I haven't a clue how to use this phone' or cutting someone off mid-sentence are signs of incompetence that won't do you or your organisation any good.

7. Never let your voice show negative emotions like anger, apathy, frustration, or lack of respect or cynicism – it will be picked up immediately, and again give a negative impression. You can't placate with a wry look or a smile over the phone line.

8. Don't use the office phone for long personal calls. It ties up the line when customers might want to get through. Some companies even ban personal phone calls or ask their employees to use a pay phone for the absolutely necessary ones.

How should I speak on the phone?

Talking is something the majority of us do without conscious thought. We open our mouths and words come out – sometimes not altogether cogently! To use the telephone well, you need to consider what you are saying – and how you are saying it.

The mechanics of talking include volume, pitch, pronunciation, and speed. To produce clear sounds you need to use a lot of your body – your back should be straight and your chest clear for breathing, your throat muscles, jaw and lips need to be relaxed (but not dribbling). Clench your teeth together and read this paragraph again out loud. It will sound like a parrot is speaking.

To avoid any confusion from interference on the line, make sure you pronounce all your words very clearly. Don't slur words or miss out the sounds of vowels or consonants.

> 'He'll probly 'ave 'm in stock.'

Speak slightly slower than normal to allow the listener to assimilate your words, and take notes. Adding pauses allows the listener to interject, or make a sign that they have understood what you have been saying.

If you are providing data – names and numbers, such as an address and postcode – if there is possible confusion use the phonetic code to make yourself clear…

That is C L E A R – Charlie, Lima, Echo, Alpha, Romeo.

The phonetic alphabet

A	Alpha	N	November
B	Bravo	O	Oscar
C	Charlie	P	Papa
D	Delta	Q	Quebec
E	Echo	R	Romeo
F	Foxtrot	S	Sierra
G	Golf	T	Tango
H	Hotel	U	Uniform
I	India	V	Victor
J	Juliet	W	Whisky
K	Kilo	X	Xray
L	Lima	Y	Yankee
M	Mike	Z	Zulu

For numbers, recognise that five and nine can sound similar – the police say 'fife' and 'nina' to make the difference obvious. It is clearer to use the American 'zero' than to say 'oh' for naught.

What you say and the tone you use gives the person you are speaking to an idea of your personality. Aim to express ideas clearly – avoiding complex sentences or words. Make sure that you are providing accurate information that is factually correct. It is also important to sound courteous and sincere. The words you use and the tone of your voice will convey emotions, often without you realising it.

Say the following sentence out loud in a monotone:

'I've got a copy of the report you wanted.'

What impression are you giving? Does it sound as if it was a real pain to get the report? Now try again and aim to sound friendly, attentive and sincere – notice how your intonation goes up and down.

What are listening skills?

Many people think that the responsibility for clear communication is with the speaker, and the hearer just passively takes in noise. In fact, listening well needs much more concentration than talking. Good communication requires active listening skills – particularly over the phone when you can't see body language or facial expressions to help read the message.

For a conversation to take place, and information to be exchanged without misunderstandings, listening involves hearing the words, assimilating them and interpreting meaning, checking, responding and confirming.

Hearing

'Good morning, does your company provide on-site car valeting services?'

(The simple answer is 'yes' or 'no' – but that's not very helpful and could lose potential new business.)

Assimilating and interpreting

This is not a random curiosity call. The caller has a dirty car, which they need cleaning urgently. I wonder how filthy it really is, and how quickly they need it tidied up. School holidays have just ended – this could be serious.

Checking

'Yes, we provide a range of services from a basic bodywork wash, wax and polish to a full internal valet, with upholstery dry-cleaning and polishing. We can clean your car on site,

or you can deliver it to our workshops for the
day. What level of service do you require?'

Responding and confirming

'I can arrange a full valet service at your
offices tomorrow for £75. Would you like to
make a booking?'

Listening well provides many benefits.

❏ It encourages others to listen well too, and improves relationships,
because the other person realises you are concentrating on them.

❏ It ensures that you get as much information as possible to solve
problems and make decisions.

❏ It improves your understanding of people so you can know what
motivates them.

Tips on active listening

1. Avoid distractions like background noise, interruptions from other
people or trying to read something or work on your computer at
the same time as listening.

2. Make sure you are comfortable. Don't sit at an odd angle or perch
on the edge of a desk.

3. Make notes – over 50% of the words we hear are forgotten within
a few minutes.

4. Don't interrupt, but make positive noises to show you are still
conscious – 'Uhuh, mmm, yes, I see'.

5. Concentrate. It's terribly easy to let your mind go off and do any of
the following while someone else is talking. *Don't:*

✖ think about how you're going to respond before they've
finished their query – what advice or information you want to
give rather than what they are asking for

✖ make judgements ('This person is a bit silly')

9

✖ worry about what they think of you, or whether you'll be able to help

✖ get impatient for the speaker to finish because you can't help, you are bored, or you know the answer and want to get the call over with

✖ get distracted because something that has been said reminds you of something else you have to do.

If you find yourself drifting, focus back on the words the caller is saying – write them down to help.

6. Check your understanding by asking questions and repeating key points.

7. Confirm your understanding by summarising.

How do I use questions?

There are four types of questions that are extremely useful if you are making or handling a call: closed, open, probing and reflective questions. Learning to use questions well gives you much greater control of the conversation – and helps avoid misunderstandings.

1. Closed questions
Closed questions are phrased so they require a 'yes' or 'no' answer. They are used to confirm information, or end a conversation.

> 'Am I speaking to the right person?'

> 'Is the price you have given me inclusive of VAT?'

> 'Can I call you back with the information tomorrow?'

2. Open questions
Open questions are used to find out more information.

> 'Would you tell me more about your query?'

> 'What exactly are the objectives of the project?'

> 'How do you think we may be able to help you?'

3. Probing questions

Probing questions explore answers more fully.

> 'You mentioned that you were unhappy with the previous service – could you tell me more about the problems that arose?'

> 'Could you explain in more detail what you hope a new office postal service could provide?'

4. Reflective questions

Reflective questions check understanding by repeating back what you have heard.

> 'So, I understand you want to find a holiday in the Caribbean in February for four adults for less than £500?'

How do I use telephone equipment well?

While listening and questioning skills are extremely important, actually knowing how to use the telephone equipment is essential for creating a professional impression of your company – and yourself.

Offices have increasingly complicated phone systems – with many features that can save time, or end up with the caller in confusion if you don't know how to make the technology work.

Check what facilities are available on your own workplace phone system, and make sure you know how to use them.

Make external and internal calls

Some systems only activate an external line if you dial 9 first. Some companies have quick dial numbers to other offices that they are in contact with frequently.

Store frequently used numbers in memory

If you call some numbers frequently, programme them in, rather than looking them up each time you need to dial. (NB It's not very professional if your stored numbers include your bookie, or the entire Saturday soccer team.)

Transfer calls to another extension

Learn how to transfer calls to a colleague if they will be able to handle a question you can't deal with.

Use the re-dial function

If you have dialled a number and it is engaged, most phones will remember the number and re-dial at the touch of a button.

Forward calls if you are busy, or away from your desk

Don't let a caller hear a busy signal or ringing phone. Automatically divert calls to another person or voicemail.

Use mute

If you are on the phone and unavoidably interrupted – apologise, ask the person to wait, and press the mute button so they don't overhear your conversation. Ensure you know how to get the caller back and don't cut them off accidently.

Use hands-free and speaker phone

Some phones have in-built speakers and microphones so you can carry on a conversation without having to anchor a handset to your ear with a hand or contorted shoulder. This shouldn't be used in an open plan office, but can be very useful if you have some privacy and need to review a document or take extensive notes while speaking. Note that it can create an echo, so don't move around a lot or go far from the phone. Also ensure that the caller knows you are using it and they don't have any objections.

Use a headset

An alternative to a speaker phone is a headset which contains ear-pieces and a microphone close to your mouth, so you don't need to disturb the people around you with the sound of your conversation. Some receptionists use this device to keep their hands free and be able to answer the phone quickly.

Adjust volume and ringer volume

It's completely off-putting to say to the person you are speaking to 'sorry, can't hear you' if you can adjust the volume on your own handset. Learn how to adjust the ringer volume too, so you can hear it but it doesn't paralyse the people around you each time your phone rings.

Record conversations

There are very few conversations that need to be recorded and your company will have a policy on this. Learn how to use the facility, and if appropriate tell the person you are speaking to that the conversation will be recorded.

Use call waiting

Some phones will tell you if another caller is trying to get through while you are on the phone, and allow you to switch between calls. Always tell the person you are speaking to that you have another call – and either end the conversation or ask them to accept a wait so you can take it.

Reminder calls

You can set reminder calls to help manage your time, for instance to warn you of a meeting or deadline.

Timing calls

Some advanced handsets will tell you how long you have been on the phone. If you don't have this facility – put a clock near your desk and refer to it to help keep the conversation short and focused.

Set up three-way calls and conferencing

Teleconferencing, or holding meetings by phone, is discussed on page 39. Make sure you know how to set them up technically before you organise one!

Use voicemail or answering services

Voicemail is both a bane and blessing, and will be covered on page 18. Make sure you know how to operate it before you start relying on the facility.

3. How do I handle callers?

Earlier we pointed out how important handling telephone calls well is for businesses. The impression you give in the first ten seconds of a phone call will very likely determine how the caller views you and your company for all time.

You have probably had bad experiences trying to get information about a product or service – are any of these familiar?

1. The phone doesn't get answered – it just rings and rings.

2. The person answering the phone speaks so quickly you can't understand them.

3. You get transferred between six different people and spend useless minutes listening to an electronic version of Greensleeves.

4. The person who answers seems bad tempered and rude, and won't help you.

5. You get cut off.

6. You leave a message and no one calls you back.

7. There is so much background noise you can't hear what is being said.

It feels as if the time spent trying to contact a company is wasted, so don't allow any of these to happen to the person calling you – or be prepared to speak to someone who is a little annoyed!

How do I answer the telephone?

Some companies have established policies on how to answer the phone – make sure you find out what the standards are. For instance, banks often don't give out staff names, but many other companies insist that you introduce yourself.

Preparation

Make sure you know enough about your company to handle enquiries. Have a staff list available, so you can transfer calls or ask colleagues for information. When you start a new job, ask your manager or colleagues to brief you on the type of calls that are received, and how they are handled.

Make sure you know which calls you should deal with, and which ones are handled by your manager or specialists. For instance, in most companies enquiries from journalists are forwarded to a specialist in the marketing department.

Keep a list of useful numbers by your phone – for general enquiries, marketing, sales, accounts etc. Many companies have internal phone lists and this should be kept near your phone.

Always have a notepad and pen handy – not for doodling but to take notes and messages.

The phone rings

Stop whatever task you were working on, and swallow that mouthful of tea or bite of cream bun (and don't refill your mouth until the call has ended!)

Smile, and relax your face muscles.

Don't pick up the phone in the middle of a conversation with someone in the office, and keep the caller waiting while you finish your sentence.

Pick up the handset within four to five rings.

Start with a greeting, such as 'Good morning' or 'Good afternoon' – this helps the caller get used to the sound of your voice before they can actually hear what you're saying. Then state your department or company, your name and give the caller a prompt.

> 'Good morning, Editorial Department, Page
> Turner speaking. Can I help you?'

Talk clearly and sound sincere – not busy, interrupted or flustered.

Listen to the caller

Write down the caller's name immediately and make notes on the query – don't expect to remember it. Listen actively to the reason for the call, and encourage the caller to talk with questions – who, what, where, when, how.

Use the caller's name when speaking to them.

> 'How can I help you, Mr Simian?'

Clarify exactly what they are trying to find out. Handle the request efficiently. Business calls are made with a purpose, the person on the telephone needs to find something out, or make an arrangement.

> 'So, if I understand you correctly, you want to place a
> wholesale order for bananas.'

Provide an answer. If you are 100% sure you know the answer to their question, give it to them immediately. If you're not sure, don't guess or make something up. Take a message and say what action will be taken and by when.

> 'I will check the current market price, and stock levels
> in produce, and get back to you today.'

Take responsibility for their satisfaction – so if you can't help, make sure the customer knows you will find someone who can.

> 'I'm sorry our warehouse stock is full of advance
> orders. Can I give you the telephone number of our
> suppliers to contact directly?'

How do I use voicemail and take messages?

With increasing use of technology and flatter organisational structures there are far fewer support roles within companies – such as secretaries or call centres. This means that you need to be proficient at taking messages and using voicemail or other telephone answering systems.

A favourite practical joke in offices is to put an inappropriate telephone number and name on a colleague's desk with an obscure message. (For instance, an old one used to be putting the telephone number of a zoo's aviary on a colleague's desk with the message 'Please call Mr Peacock urgently'.) This may seem very funny to the practical joker, but it can cause embarrassment and it certainly wastes your and other people's time.

Taking a message efficiently helps to give a good impression of your company, and helps your colleague to return the call well.

✖ Farrah called about the tickets.

✔ Farrah Waye called at 3pm to find out if the flight tickets to Colorado have arrived yet. Her telephone number is 0171 555 5555.

Message notepads are common stationery supply and prompt you to collect all the right details so that messages can be responded to appropriately. You should always write down…

Name of caller: _____
Company: _____
Telephone number: _____
Time of call: _____
Message: _____
_____
Action required: _____
Your name: _____

…so the person responding has all the information they need to handle the query with one phone call.

Using voicemail

Voicemail is a way of recording a personal message on your direct telephone line, if you are on the phone or away from your desk.

You should always record a greeting and your name, then invite the caller to leave a message or call another number.

Some companies insist that employees change their message daily, explaining whether they are in the office, or away, and when they will respond to the caller. If your message does include a time when you will be back, or a date, you must update it frequently. It's frustrating for callers to hear that you will be 'back in the office' on a date three days previously.

Recorded messages should be as brief as possible – but don't speak too fast, especially if you are giving an alternative number or contact name, as the caller needs a chance to write it down.

Any messages should be responded to as quickly as possible – at least within a working day.

How do I bring a call to a close?

If you are handling a telephone call that doesn't seem to be progressing – take the initiative. Direct the conversation with a closed question which has to be answered by a 'yes' or 'no'.

> 'Can I get Terry Dactile to call you back tomorrow with the details?'

> 'Shall I send you some information to help you make a decision?'

> 'Would you like to discuss the idea with your boss and get back to me?'

How do I handle complaints and difficult calls?

It's not unusual for customers to phone a company with a complaint or problem. They are probably angry and frustrated. You can help reduce their upset by dealing with the call well – or you can make it ten times worse!

Things to do:

✔ Be personal – provide your name, and get the caller's name so you can address them directly.

✔ Volunteer to help, don't wait to be asked. 'Ms Stake, how can I help?'

✔ Allow the caller let of steam – don't interrupt, and encourage them to provide all the details.

✔ Take them seriously – repeat back what they have told you to verify you understand the problem. 'Ms Stake, I understand that you think £10,000 has been wrongly debited from your account – is that right?'

✔ Offer sympathy but don't get too involved. 'I can understand why you are feeling annoyed', not 'That's *awful*, you must have been in a right panic, I would scream if it happened to me.'

✔ Summarise what you have agreed to do. 'Ms Stake, I will look into your account straight away and telephone you back by the end of the day.'

✔ If more problems turn up – call them first, don't wait for a second angry call. 'Ms Stake, I've just looked and it seems another £5000 has been debited from your account, so I will investigate that too.'

✔ Act on the problem as quickly as you can – speak to colleagues or write out notes, summarising the situation.

Things to avoid:

✘ Don't attempt to reason or make excuses while someone is really angry.

✘ Don't suggest a solution if you don't have all the facts.

✘ Don't blame others or look for sympathy. 'I'm only a trainee and everyone else is out at lunch' sounds pathetic – especially to someone who already thinks badly of your organisation.

✘ Don't get angry or upset yourself – stay calm.

✘ Don't agree to do something you don't have authority to do.

4. How do I make telephone calls?

Everyone knows how to use the phone – you just pick up the handset and dial, then say the first thing that comes into your head. While this is an active approach, it's often not an effective one if you have a business problem to solve and want to do it by phone.

For instance, you might be calling up a travel agent to find out about the best way to get to Italy, contacting a hotel to organise a meeting, booking places on a training course, or querying an invoice.

Some phone calls are easier to handle than others, because you know exactly who to call and what to ask, for example:

❏ Finding out the time of trains from an enquiry line.

> 'Good morning, can you tell me the departure and arrival times for trains from Liverpool to Manchester on Monday morning, arriving at about 10am?'

❏ Booking a restaurant table.

> 'Good afternoon, I would like to book at table for five, for lunch next Tuesday at 1pm.'

Where you need to find out more complex information or solve a problem, to use time well and avoid the embarrassment and potential damage of giving a poor impression you need to take more care:

❏ Prepare for the call

❏ Find the right person to speak to – *Who*

❏ Introduce yourself and your question – *What*

❏ Ensure they are able to speak to you – *When*

❏ Speak clearly and calmly, and use questioning and listening skills to get to a successful outcome.

What problems can happen when making calls?

Phone calls can be extremely frustrating. You have a problem to solve, a deadline to meet, and somehow the fates transpire to fight against your priorities:

❏ You don't know who to speak to.

❏ The number is busy or disconnected.

❏ You get stuck in a voicemail system or on call waiting, passed between different people.

❏ The person you speak to is uninterested, unhelpful, rude or stupid.

❏ The information you have so far is wrong, so you have to start again.

What preparation do I need to do to make telephone calls?

1. Decide what you are trying to achieve – what information do you need to find out, what messages do you need to transmit?

2. Write down notes and a checklist – the name and number of the person calling and the information you have so far, and the questions you want to ask.

3. Have any additional paperwork that you may need to refer to handy.

4. Have a notebook and pen available for making notes.

5. Choose a good time of day to call. For instance, at lunch time most people are away from their desks.

6. Make sure you won't be interrupted, and there isn't any loud background noise – radio, building works or an office meeting.

7. Relax and breathe deeply, make sure you are sitting in a comfortable position. Smile and loosen up your face muscles.

8. Have a clock in sight so you are aware of the time spent on the phone.

9. Be prepared for the call to be unsuccessful first time round – if the person you speak to is busy arrange another time to call back, or be ready to leave a message if you reach another person or voicemail.

10. Concentrate on listening to the person who picks up the phone, and work on building a rapport with them.

A true case study

In researching this book, I called a supplier of telephone services in the UK. I wanted to find out how many business telephone numbers there are, and how many calls are made everyday. This is what happened.

First I checked the telephone directory, which provided a freephone number for general enquiries. I called it, and explained my question to the operator.

The operator transferred me to the publicity department. Unfortunately that person's voicemail indicated he was on holiday for two weeks – but supplied a colleague's name and number to call. The name wasn't clear, and it wasn't a freephone number.

I dialled anyway. The person who answered the phone seemed annoyed that the call had been put through to her, so transferred me to a colleague.

I explained my question again. The second person I spoke to was more interested in how he had been dumped with the call than helping and said, 'You need to talk to finance. I'll put you through.'

After several seconds of music on hold a voice said, 'Hello.' I explained my query again. The voice said, 'This is switchboard, I'll just put you through.' More call waiting.

A relatively welcoming voice answered the phone then. Unfortunately it was the customer support department for domestic users and she was completely baffled by my questions. She did however make a suggestion. 'Why don't you call the business user customer support line?'

I hung up, looked up the number and dialled again. A voicemail menu gave me an option for general enquiries. When I explained for the fifth time what I wanted to know the customer assistance specialist was very specific. 'No. Can't help you.' I asked for suggestions – a marketing department or external research agency. 'No, sorry, don't know anything about that.' I thanked her for her help as politely as I could and put the phone down.

So, I rang a competitor, to find out if they could be more useful – and to change my telephone account, regardless of cost or inconvenience.

How do I get the right person?

The case study on the previous page illustrates how frustrating and difficult it can be to find the right person to speak to if you have a general enquiry (and how companies can lose business by mishandling callers). You will probably speak to a receptionist or operator first – and they have limited time to deal with each call. They may also have limited understanding of roles and departments if it is a big company. If the receptionist is a temp or a new member of staff they will be even more confused by a complicated request.

Don't go into huge details about your enquiry with the first person in the company who answers the phone, but choose some key words to help them find the right person to speak to you. Make the request brief and relevant, and be patient, until you are talking to the right person.

First sentence:

- A. 'I want to speak to someone about my invoice number 3245 dated 14th July, for computer equipment, because it is wrong and my boss is steaming.'
  (26 words)

- B. 'I want to speak to your accounts department.'
  (8 words)

Second sentence:

- A. 'I really need to speak to someone about my invoice number 3245 dated 14th July, for computer equipment, because it is wrong and my boss is steaming, can you deal with it?'
  (32 words)

- B. 'I need to query an invoice, can you help?'
  (9 words)

Third sentence:

A. 'You are the THIRD person I've spoken to and I have
    a big problem with an invoice – my boss is absolutely
    furious. It's invoice number 3245 dated 14th July, for
    computer equipment, and the company name is IRE
    Ltd.'
    (39 words)

B. I'd like to question invoice number 3245, the account
    name is IRE Ltd. Can you help me?
    (17 words)

Who will get the best response in the shortest time – A or B?

How do I introduce myself and my subject?

'What ho,' I said
'What ho,' said Monty
'What ho! What ho!'
'What ho! What ho! What ho!'
After that it seemed rather difficult to go on with the
conversation.

PJ Wodehouse, *My Man Jeeves* 1919

When you have contacted the right person, answer the first two
questions *Who* and *What* as you introduce yourself.

'Hello, my name is Roz Berry, I work for a farming
cooperative and I would like to find out more about
your new range of organic fertilisers.'

Be clear, concise and courteous. Start by ensuring that the person
you are speaking to has time to deal with your call.

'Is this a convenient time for you to answer some
questions?'

If the answer is no, accept it with good grace, and offer alternatives.

'Could I call back at another time?'

or   'Could someone else help me?'

When you have established that the person you are speaking to will handle your enquiry be as precise as possible about what you want to find out.

> 'I heard about your products from a contact, and have seen your latest catalogue. We are setting up a new greenhouse to grow soft fruits and want to use organic methods. Can you tell me about the products you have that would be appropriate? I need to get some idea of costs because I must put a budget together by the end of the week.'

5. What other skills should I know about when using the telephone?

How do I make sales calls?

The purpose of a sales call is to interest someone in a product or service, and persuade them to buy it.

There are three types of sales calls you might need to make:

1. Service calls – where an existing customer is contacted
2. Follow-up calls – where a person has made an enquiry
3. Cold calls – where an individual is contacted out of the blue.

Telephone selling – or telesales – is associated most with cold calls and has a bad reputation in the UK – not without some justification, as many callers are untrained or badly prepared.

Successful telephone sales people:

❑ Listen to the person they are speaking to and identify the best approach to develop empathy.

❑ Quickly establish if the person they are speaking to is likely to make a purchase – do they have the money, the authority to buy, and a need? If not then time is better spent talking to someone else.

❏ Offer a solution. Find a need or a problem that features of the product or service will solve, and provide factual information to make the point clearly. Buyers want products or services that will save time or money, solve problems or improve situations.

❏ Handle objections through acknowledgement and questions.

❏ 'Close'– ask for commitment, for example for an appointment or order, or the opportunity to call again.

Each call can have more than one objective.

Type of call	Objectives
Service	Sort out a problem
	Build up a positive image
	Get a new order
	Offer other services
Enquiry	Arrange an appointment
	Send on information
	Find out about the requirements and needs
	Get additional contacts
Cold call	Promote a company's name and its product or service
	Agree to send information
	Make an appointment
	Offer other services

Let's take an example. Bill is making a cold call to a company to introduce his firm's new range of office furniture. He has found out the name of the office manager, Ben Dandsway, and this is one way his side of the conversation might go:

Introduce and listen	'Good morning Mr Dandsway. My name is Bill Tulast from Substantial Furnishings Ltd.

Establish authority and need	'Is your company considering office expansion at the moment? Are you responsible for furnishings and fittings?'
Offer a solution	'It may be that we can help you with some very economical and hardwearing desk units, if you are on a tight budget – would that be of interest?'
Handle objections	'I understand that you are happy with your current supplier, but If I could show you that our prices are lower, and delivery times are very short, would you be interested?'
Close – get commitment	'You are obviously busy at the moment – could I send you some information and call back in a week? What would be a convenient time?

The conversation could have gone many different ways – Bill could have found out that Ben Dandsway was not the decision-maker, so he might ask for another contact.

Establish authority and need	'Can you tell me who is responsible for your company's furniture requirements?'

Mr Dandsway might have used the objection that the company didn't have any budget for new furniture, so Bill might offer another service:

Offer a solution	'Substantial Furnishings will also recondition desk units and chairs and ensure they comply with current Health & Safety regulations. Would that be of interest?'

How do I call people overseas?

It can be a bit daunting to call someone in another country. The combination of cultural differences, foreign languages and poor line quality can multiply misunderstandings.

1. The first thing to do is check time differences so that you call during normal working hours in the other country. For example, much of Europe is only one or two hours ahead of the UK, so calling at between 9am and 4pm would probably be OK. Whereas New York is five hours behind, so don't phone until after 1pm to catch them after 9 o'clock in the morning. Australia is 12 hours ahead, so if you phone at lunch time it would be the middle of the night there – think about sending a fax instead. (But only to an office. You will not get a positive response if you have woken a potential customer at 2am!)

2. If you are phoning a country that does not have English as a first language, and you don't speak the language yourself, learn how to make the correct greeting in the right language, and how to ask for the person you wish to speak to.

French	*Good-day*	*Bonjour*
Spanish	*Good morning*	*Buenos dias*
	Good afternoon	*Buenos tardes*
German	*Good morning*	*Guten morgen*
	Good evening	*Guten abend*

3. Learn the phrase to ask if the person you are talking to speaks English. For example:

French	*Parlez-vous Anglaise?*
Spanish	*Habla Inglis?*
German	*Sprechen sie Englisch?*

And learn the phrase for 'No, I don't speak English' so you understand the answer!

4. If you can't communicate, end the conversation politely, if possible saying in the other language that you will phone back later, and then find a translator to help you with the call.

5. If the person does speak English, speak politely and concisely – as you should anyway. Don't shout or slow down your speech to a snail's pace – neither will make you more comprehensible and it is patronising to the other person.

6. When you finish the call, if the other person has had to speak in English, it is polite to learn the phrase 'Thank you for your help. Goodbye' in the appropriate language.

Don't be embarrassed to use a few foreign phrases – even if you have the worst accent in the world, it is appreciated by others who do make the effort to speak in your language.

How do I use a mobile phone?

Mobile telephones are extremely useful communication devices for business people who travel, or are away from their office frequently. They can also be a source of intense irritation for other people – even blinding rage – if used inappropriately. Learn and follow the etiquette – which is a mixture of basic politeness and common sense.

If you have a mobile phone:

❏ Make sure it has a suitable message service, so that messages can be easily left by the caller and retrieved by you.

❏ Switch it off when you are unable to speak – for instance in meetings or when driving.

❏ Unless it's absolutely necessary switch it off in restaurants and other social venues. Some restaurants ban mobile telephones now.

❏ Keep conversations short and to the point.

❏ Try to find somewhere private and quiet before making a call.

❑ Don't make a call if the reception is bad or your batteries are low –
it creates frustration for the person on the other end of the line.

If you are calling a mobile phone number:

❑ Find out where the receiver is and if they are able to talk.

❑ Be prepared to leave a message if the phone is engaged or
switched off.

❑ Recognise that the person you are speaking to may be in public –
so might not want to have a long, detailed or contentious
conversation.

How do I use the phone when looking for a job?

However hard it seems, you will need to use the telephone on job
searches to:

❑ apply for advertised vacancies

❑ call organisations about vacancies.

If you are applying for an advertised vacancy, telephoning as soon as
possible can give you some advantages. You are unlikely to arrange
an interview immediately, but you can get an application form quickly
or ensure that the recruiter is expecting your CV.

Do your preparation

1. Go through the advertisement and work out how your skills and
experience match their specification.

2. Prepare a checklist of questions about the job, to show you are
interested and to be better prepared for the interview.

3. Have a pen and paper handy to take notes.

4. Arrange to call from a location where you won't be interrupted or
cut off. If you need to use a mobile phone or phone box make sure
you have enough credits on your phone card and the line is clear.

Handle the call professionally

1. Be specific. Don't say 'I'm calling about the job' say 'I'm responding to your advertisement in the *Sunday Times*, reference 2341, for a sales executive.'

2. If you don't get through immediately, leave a message but don't expect to be called back – say you will try again, and do so.

3. When you get through to the right person give your name, and get the name of the person you are speaking to so you can address them directly. 'Good morning, my name is Eva Green, who am I speaking to?'

4. Ask relevant questions: details about the job not included in the advertisement, such as where is the office located, is it a new role, and how should you make a formal application?

5. Ask for an application form, or if you are really interested ask if you can fax your CV to them quickly – and don't forget to ask for their fax number.

6. Thank the person on the phone for their help and time.

7. After the call send off the required information as soon as possible with a covering letter.

Contacting organisations directly

You may have heard about a company – through a friend or newspaper article – and thought, 'I'd like to work for them.' Of course you can send off a bland letter with your CV to the personnel department, but a phone call can be much more effective.

1. Do some research and preparation – find out exactly what the company does and decide how you could fit in – and what contribution you could make. You'll need to sell yourself a bit so confidence and enthusiasm are important.

2. When you get through to the right person, ask if it is convenient for them to talk.

3. Say why you are interested and what contribution you could make;

for example, 'I have two years' experience of administration in a production company.'

4. Ask for help – most people are flattered by a request for their personal assistance and are unlikely to cut you short. 'I would really appreciate your advice on... who I should be speaking to... how your company goes about recruitment... where I could send a CV or letter for future reference.'

Where people go wrong in telephoning to apply for jobs

If you are skilled at using the phone, you should avoid the obvious pitfalls. However, too often people make simple mistakes in the hurry to get the call over with. Think before you call – you can miss potential opportunities if you are guilty of any of these:

❑ No preparation, not knowing enough about the organisation.

❑ Hanging on too long to speak to someone who is obviously busy. They are not going to deal with a speculative phone call willingly if they have just finished another call.

❑ Leaving messages asking for a call back when the person doesn't know you – they may think it's a sales call.

❑ Leaving a contact number which is not answered well – a jokey answer machine, a social club or your own phone but you don't remember that you made contact in the first place.

What are telephone interviews?

Sometimes first interviews for some jobs are conducted over the telephone. This may happen if the applicant lives a long way from the work site and travel is inconvenient, or by agencies of busy firms who are shortlisting. Generally telephone interviews are a 'weeding-out' process. You are unlikely to make so good an impression you will win a job, but you can easily do yourself out of the next interview stage by handling a call badly.

All the rules of good telephone techniques apply. Sit up straight, smile, don't eat, drink or smoke. Remember this will be a longer and more formal call than normal business conversations. It is more like a meeting and you should be prepared with all your paperwork, a copy of the job advertisement and your response, and your CV. If you are asked for basic information it will be there at your fingertips and you won't waste the interviewer's time trying to work out dates based on your grandfather's 85th birthday party or the year America last hosted the World Cup.

The interview may be conducted by appointment – at an arranged time at your home. If so, there is no excuse for not being prepared. Also make sure you can take the call in a private room, with no domestic background noise. Answer it yourself – don't let the labrador or the resident four-year-old pick up the phone and confuse the caller.

However you normally answer your home phone, it is a good idea to speak as you would at work, with a greeting and your name. This will get the conversation off to a professional start. Answer all questions clearly and concisely – don't waffle, and don't interrupt.

At the end of the call you may be told if you have been successful or not. If you are not invited to the next interview, politely ask the caller if they can give you any advice on why not. Listen to the answer – don't argue with it – as it this feedback can help you improve your technique for next time.

How do I save time using the phone?

If it is you making the phone call, you should be able to structure the conversation in advance, and keep it to a minimum length. Here are some guidelines:

❑ Have a good reason for phoning – don't make a business call on the spur of the moment or on the basis of a flimsy idea. Even if you are just 'networking', which is about keeping in touch with people, you should have a focus for your conversation.

❑ Prepare for the call and have all the relevant information to hand.

❑ Have paper and pen ready to take notes.

❑ Keep a timer or clock on your desk. Being aware of how long your phone calls take will help you keep them brief and concise.

❑ Keep the conversation to the point. If you become sidetracked, use a reflective question to get back to the main issue. 'So you can confirm delivery of our order by 11am on Monday?' Thank the other person for their help and end the call.

❑ If you don't get through, leave a clear message that someone can respond to easily. If your message is complicated or private, find out the best time to ring back.

❑ If you have a lot of calls to make, prepare notes for all of them and tackle them together at a given time in the day.

If you are receiving the call:

❑ Answer clearly with your name or department.

❑ Listen carefully to the caller to understand their reason for phoning.

❑ If you cannot answer the question immediately, transfer the caller to someone you know who can, or take a message.

❑ Don't keep the caller on hold while you search for information or the relevant person. If it is likely to take more than 20–30 seconds to find the answer and get them back off hold, take a message and call them back.

❑ Use the same techniques for keeping the call short and focused.

What is teleconferencing?

Teleconferencing is holding telephone meetings between people in different locations. Run properly teleconferences can save a great deal of travel time and be set up much more quickly than physical meetings.

Simple meetings between two locations can be run with speaker phones – where a handset in each office is used to hold a conversation between two groups of people. More sophisticated facilities exist to 'patch' in callers from many locations.

If you are organising a teleconference meeting:

❑ Make sure the technology works – do a dry run with administration staff or other colleagues.

❑ Ensure all participants have the same documents to refer to, in advance.

❑ Start the meeting by introducing everyone and asking them to speak to check transmission.

❑ Guide the conversation. 'We are here to discuss the proposal from Wentworth Prison on a weekend retreat and management training programme. You will have received the document last week, so I will ask you each in turn to provide comments, by calling you by name. To help aid everyone else, as you start to speak please say your name and office location, and please be as brief as possible.'

❑ Stop side conversations and rabbiters.

❑ Take notes and summarise after each person has spoken.

If you are participating in a teleconference organised by someone else, speak when asked and avoid interrupting others. Keep a note of any queries you have and briefly state them when asked.

What are telecommuting and teleworking?

Telecommuters

More and more companies are deciding that big head offices housing all their staff is not cost effective and that many roles can be carried out effectively from home bases. This saves employees the cost and time of commuting.

Telecommuters are employees, contractors or freelancers who visit their company offices infrequently and are in contact with their manager and colleagues primarily by phone and email.

Examples include:

❑ Field sales people – based in regions away from the main office

❑ Writers

❑ Computer programmers.

Telecommuters need to be comfortable at communicating by phone to sort out problems and discuss work with their colleagues – but most of their time is spent travelling or working on their own.

Teleworkers

Teleworkers are employees or freelancers who carry out telephone-based jobs from home. Telephone research programmes are often carried out by teleworkers who are provided with questionnaires and contact numbers to call over a period of time. This type of work is often done in the evenings.

6. Where can I find out more?

Who could I contact?

BT Freephone number for a recorded message on telephone skills.
0800 800876

OFTEL: 0171 634 8700

The Telephone Users' Association: 0181 445 0096.

There are a range of training organisations that run courses on telephone sales skills – check in your local phone directory.

What publications could I look at?

Telephone directories – local listings, business pages and guides provide a wealth of information and help.

The business section in your local library should offer a range of books or tapes on telephone skills and foreign languages.

Making that call: Winning tactics for 101 difficult telephone conversations, Iain Maitland, Kogan Page 1997

Better business by phone: A guide to effective telebusiness management, Valerie O'Dea, Macmillan 1998

Tough telephoning: Mastering business on the telephone, David M Martin, Pitman 1996